The Lord Has Need of YOU
Jesus' Last Days on This Earth

A read alone - read aloud book

Author- Connie Wohlford
Illustrator- Lesley James

Though the parallel story with the donkeys, Elpis, Kavod, and Gil is fictional, *The Lord Has Need of You* depicts the true account of Jesus' triumphal entry into Jerusalem, His death, burial, resurrection, and ascension, adapted from the following Scripture passages taken from the New King James version of the Bible:

Matthew 21:1-3, 9, 12; Matthew 22:36-39; Luke 22:19; Matthew 26:39; John 19:30, 20:1-17, 19-22; Mark 16:15-16; Acts 1:8, 11.

GLOSSARY
Elpis (pronounced el-peese`) - Greek for hope.
Kavod – Hebrew for glory; honor; respect.
Gil – Hebrew for joy; happiness.
Yeshua is Jesus' Hebrew name – means to rescue; to deliver. *Jesus* is His name in Greek.
Hosanna - expresses adoration, praise and joy. <> Means "Hooray for salvation! It's coming! It's here! Salvation! Salvation!" – John Piper- **www.desiringgod.org**
Passover - the Jewish festival that celebrates the deliverance of the Israelites from Egyptian slavery.
Caiaphas - the Jewish high priest who was believed to have organized the plot to kill Jesus.
Rabboni – respected teacher or master.

All rights reserved. This book may not be reproduced in whole or in part, in any matter whatsoever, without written permission of the author with the exception of brief quotations within book reviews and articles.

Copyright © Connie Wohlford 2019
ISBN: 978-1-687536-10-5

Dedication

I want to dedicate *The Lord Has Need of YOU* to my eight amazing grandchildren. Though they are now teenagers, they're the ones who inspired all of my children's stories and books. It's my greatest desire that each of them knows and loves Jesus well.

Also, I dedicate this book to our Savior/Messiah, Jesus. Without Him the story would not exist. He put the stories in my heart and gave me the confidence to actually pursue publication. When it is God's idea, the courage to move forward is not so hard to muster. Thank You, Heavenly Father.

At the sight of the stranger walking his way, Kavod leaned against his mama's belly. Suddenly the man reached to grab the colt! His mama, Elpis, raised her head and with a gaping toothy lunge, grabbed the thief's wrist.

The startled man jerked back, writhing in pain and ran away.

Elpis said, "He won't be back."

Kavod batted his eyelids, lowered his head and said, "I should have been brave and bitten him myself."

"You'll learn. You did sense his evil nature. That's a good thing.

Just then, two other strangers walked around the corner. Kavod looked at the men, stepped toward them, and raised his nose to sniff. As the man named James untied Elpis, her owner stepped from the house. Before he could speak, the second stranger, named John, spoke up and said, "The Lord has need of them."

The man in the doorway looked at the donkeys. Then he smiled at the men, nodded his head, and went back into the house.

Elpis said to Kavod, "I've seen these men before. They're friends of Jesus."

"How do you know Jesus?" asked the colt.

"I knew Jesus when I was your age. My mama still belongs to His family. You could say Jesus and I grew up together in Nazareth where I was born."

"Jesus was the kindest kid in the whole village. He would bring Mama and me treats and was nice to everyone."

"What's your mama like?" asked Kavod.

"She is always full of joy. In fact, her name is Gil which means *joy*. That was a very appropriate name when Mama had the great joy of carrying Jesus' mother, Mary, to Bethlehem.

That's where Jesus was born, and Mama was right there with them."

"I was too young to go, and I missed Mama so much. Before she left, Mama told me God would take care of me and reminded me that my name means *hope* and I needed to continue to hope that she would come home someday. And she finally did."

The four walked up to Jesus, who was sitting under an olive tree with the rest of His disciples.

Jesus stood up, wrapped His arms around Elpis' and said, "Hello Elpis—my old friend and playmate! You have a handsome, strong colt."

Elpis closed her eyes and delighted in His gentle touch. Jesus rubbed Kavod's head and ran His hand across his wide back.

Another disciple named Peter, asked, "Are you sure this colt is strong enough to carry You?"

"Yes, he'll be fine," said Jesus.

A little nervous, Kavod questioned his mama, "I've never been ridden before. Do you think I can carry Jesus?"

"You'll be fine. The Lord has need of you and has called you, so He knows you can do it. You'll have special strength—and you're stronger than you think."

Peter placed two of the disciples' cloaks on Kavod's back. The rest of the men's cloaks were laid on Elpis.

Kavod felt the weight of Jesus on his back and was unsure about taking a step. But when Jesus leaned forward and patted his neck, he knew he could do this task for the Lord.

They started walking toward the beautiful city of Jerusalem. It wasn't far and people began to gather.

More and more happy people—men, women, and children lined up along the road to see Jesus, who was called Yeshua by the Jews. Some of them put their cloaks on the road for the donkeys and disciples to walk on. They rejoiced, welcoming their Messiah.

Kavod stood up straight and tall. He tried to look as strong and regal as he could manage.

Many waved palm branches and laid them in the road to honor their Messiah as He went along.

The joyful crowd shouted, "Hosanna to the Son of David! Blessed is He Who comes in the name of the Lord! Hosanna in the highest!"

Jesus smiled and waved at the people. The multitude rejoiced that their Deliverer had finally come.

Kavod's heart leapt, sensing the great honor of carrying the King of kings on his back. Elpis was overjoyed seeing her own colt carry her beloved friend.

When they arrived at the Temple, Jesus dismounted his ride and said, "Kavod, you are good and strong—and you're well named because you have carried the Father's glory on your back. Thank you, my young friend."

Jesus rubbed Kavod's head and patted Elpis as she rested her head against his chest.

Jesus and His disciples walked toward the beautiful Temple. The donkeys lost sight of them as they entered the outer court. Inside, Jesus saw some things that upset him deeply.

Most people were there to worship God, but others were exchanging foreign coins for less than they were worth. Some shop keepers were charging too much money for items to be used in worship. Jesus saw that these merchants were stealing from people who just wanted to please God. In His eyes, they were like thieves.

He was not going to put up with this and pushed over the merchants' tables. Everyone stared in disbelief as money and merchandise spilled onto the floor, but they knew in their hearts that Jesus was right. The merchants had dishonored God and His Temple with their actions.

Then, Jesus said, "It is written, 'My house shall be called a house of prayer, but you have made it a den of thieves!'"

Jesus and His disciples walked further into the Temple complex. Blind and crippled people came to Jesus, and He healed them. Several children ran to see Him, and He greeted and blessed each one.

Later that day, Jesus and the twelve went to the nearby city of Bethany to the home of Lazarus, Martha, and Mary. There they ate and slept, always happy to visit with their friends.

Meanwhile, Kavod and Elpis were returned to their master.

For the next few days, Jesus stayed in the area of Jerusalem, spending much time in the Temple. People listened to Him teach about God and were amazed at His wisdom and His power to heal the sick. The crowds loved to listen to His stories, which helped them understand what the Kingdom of God is like.

But some of the Jewish leaders were jealous and angry because many of their fellow Jews chose to follow Jesus.

One morning, Elpis and Kavod were in the city with their master. Jesus saw His four hooved friends and walked over to pet them. The donkeys were very glad to see Jesus.

As they stood together, someone asked, "Teacher, what is the greatest commandment?"

Without hesitating, Jesus answered, "You shall love the Lord your God with all your heart, with all your soul, and with all your mind. And the second greatest commandment is, you shall love your neighbor as yourself."

The people who were against Jesus began to devise a plan to get rid of Him. They did not believe He was the Messiah and didn't want anyone else to believe either. They even bribed Judas, one of His disciples, to help them capture Him. But Jesus knew what they were up to all along.

The time had come to celebrate the Jewish holiday called Passover. Jesus and his disciples gathered in the upper room of someone's house to celebrate the feast together.

When Jesus blessed the bread and wine, he said an unusual thing: "Eat this bread and drink this wine in remembrance of Me."

His disciples had no idea this would be the last supper with their beloved friend and teacher.

That night, in a garden called Gethsemane, Jesus and His disciples, except for Judas, went to pray

Hours passed, the torches burned out, and the disciples all nodded off. But Jesus was still praying. He knew He was facing a lot of pain and suffering.

In the end, He cried out, "Oh, My Father, if it is possible, let there be another way. Nevertheless, not My will but Your will be done."

All of a sudden, the disciples were jolted awake by the clamoring of swords shattering the quiet night. They staggered to their feet and rubbed their eyes to see what was causing the commotion.

Judas led soldiers to Jesus and kissed His cheek to show the soldiers He was the one they wanted. Judas had betrayed his best friend.

The muscular soldiers grabbed Jesus and led Him away to face the high priest, Caiaphas. Jesus had been accused of breaking laws.

A few hours later, Jesus was handed over to Pontius Pilate, a Roman government official. Pilate brought Jesus before the people and asked them, "What do you want me to do with your King?"

Early that same morning, Elpis and Kavod were grazing in a pasture outside of Jerusalem. The sky was blue, and the bright sunlight invited the lilies of the field to open wide and soak in its rays.

Kavod raised his head to sniff the warm air, then said, "Mama, I have a bad feeling, and I don't know why."

Elpis looked around and said, "My dear Kavod, when you feel that way, you must pray. God knows everything, and He can comfort you and show you what to do."

The peaceful morning was interrupted by the sounds of voices stirring up in the city. Louder and louder it became. People were shouting, "Crucify Him! Crucify Him!" That was the crowd's answer to Pontius Pilate.

People started pouring out of the city seeming to focus on a man who was carrying a heavy cross. Slowly, they made their way up the hill not far from Elpis and Kavod.

The donkeys turned to each other and at the same time, said, "It's Jesus!"

The donkeys watched in horror as Jesus was nailed to a cross in between two criminals. The beautiful spring day had turned into a dreadful, sad day.

After a while, Jesus said, "It is finished!" and He died.

At that very moment, the sky darkened, and the earth shook in such a manner that the donkeys nearly fell down.

Elpis and Kavod stood watching in disbelief. There was Jesus, who had done so many good and kind things, being killed as though He were a criminal. It just didn't make sense.

The donkeys could not stop their tears.

Some of Jesus' friends took his body and laid it in a tomb which was in a beautiful garden nearby. But the beauty of the surroundings didn't take away the sadness in their hearts.

Pilate commanded that a heavy stone seal the opening of the tomb. He also ordered two Roman soldiers to guard the tomb where Jesus' body was laid.

Two days passed. Sadness and fear squeezed the hearts of Jesus' disciples and other followers. They didn't know what to do next.

Before the sun came up on the morning of the third day, Jesus' friend, Mary Magdalene, went to His tomb. She was shocked to see that the stone had been rolled away, leaving the burial place wide open.

She ran and told Peter and John. They pushed into the tomb to find the Lord's face cloth and linen burial cloth neatly folded. But there was no sign of Jesus' body. Dragging their feet, the men left and went home.

Mary was left alone. She stood sobbing and looking into the tomb where her Lord had lain.

She could not stop the tears from flowing.

Something or someone was coming into focus. There before her were two bright shining angels—one at the head and the other at the foot, where the body of Jesus had been.

One spoke up and said, "Woman, why are you weeping?"

She replied, "Because they have taken away my Lord, and I do not know where they have laid Him."

She then turned and saw someone she thought was a gardener.

The man spoke: "Why are you weeping? Who are you seeking?"

Still not recognizing Him, she said, "Sir, if you've taken Him away, please tell me."

He looked her in the eye and said, "Mary!"

Then she knew! She knew that her friend—her Savior—was standing there—ALIVE!

Thrilled with surprise, she dropped to the ground at His feet and proclaimed, "Rabboni!" which means *teacher*.

"Do not hold on to me for I have not yet ascended to My Father. Go and tell My brethren."

Later that same day, as the disciples gathered together, Jesus appeared and stood among them. They were shocked and whispered to one another, "Is this a ghost? Did he play a trick?"

But, no, this was not a ghost and Jesus wasn't playing a trick. He even let them touch Him so they could be sure. It was a miracle from God. And there He was—for real!

He showed them the wounds on His hands and feet and then said, "Peace be with you! As the Father has sent Me, I also send you."

He then breathed on them and said, "Receive the Holy Spirit."

"Go into all the world and preach this Good News to everyone—that all who believe in Me will be saved."

For several days Jesus appeared to many people throughout the city, so there were lots of people who knew for certain, Jesus was alive!

"Mama, it's the thief! But, Mama, something's different. He's changed. Now I sense good in him—not evil."

The door opened and the man of the house growled, "What do you want?"

"I've been gathering wood to give the widows. I brought some to you too and want to ask you to forgive me for all the wrong I've done to you."

"I don't believe you! Go away!" said the man, starting to shut the door.

"No—stop! Please listen! I saw Jesus! He's alive!"

"Jesus is dead! Go away!"

"No! He's alive! Many have seen Him. When I heard Him talk about God's love and forgiveness, I really listened. I watched them crucify Him, but I knew He was an innocent man. My heart broke because I knew He was dying for me. I deserved to be the one on the cross! He did that for me—and for you—and for all of us. All I could do was weep and thank God for the sacrifice of Jesus. He is our Messiah!"

"My brother, please forgive me. I'll try to make everything up to you. Jesus is alive! God raised Him from the dead! Please believe me."

"I believe you! Do you know where He is? I want to see Him."

"I think we can find Him. Let's go."

Several days later, when Jesus and His disciples were all together, He gave them some final encouragement and instructions.

"Soon you will be baptized with the Holy Spirit and receive power. You shall be My witnesses in Jerusalem and to the ends of the earth."

Then, as they watched, Jesus was taken up into a cloud. The men stood there, not knowing quite what to think. But their hearts were full of peace and joy.

As they stared toward Heaven, two angels wearing white clothing stood next to them.

One of the angels said, "Men of Galilee, why do you stand gazing up into Heaven? This same Jesus, who was taken up from you into Heaven, will return again, in like manner, just as you saw Him go."

Epilogue

Like the young donkey, Kavod, we're each given a task by the Lord. God has it all figured out beforehand. Even if we are not strong enough, or smart enough, or rich enough, we should step out into the thing He has called us to do.

Jesus said, "My grace is sufficient for you, for My power is made perfect in weakness" (1 Corinthians 12:9).

Let's do what Kavod did and take that first step, knowing that Jesus is right there with us to help us complete the task. In the story, the disciple said, about the donkeys, "The Lord has need of them." Well, the Lord has need of each of us. Let's not let Him down.

Also, each one of us, who is His follower, is instructed by Jesus to spread the Good News. That news is that God sent Jesus to Earth to live among people and then to take the punishment that we each deserved by dying on the cross for our sins.

By the power of God, Jesus rose from the dead and is now in Heaven preparing an eternal home for us.

When we believe all these things about Jesus and invite Him to live in our hearts, we are born-again and become members of God's own family. That's when the Holy Spirit comes to live in us to help us in all areas of our lives.

If you have not invited Jesus into your heart and would like to do so, just talk to God with this prayer: *"God, I believe that Jesus is Your Son just like the Bible says. Jesus, I'm inviting You to come into my heart and save me from my sins and to help me live for You for the rest of my life. Thank You. In Jesus' Name—Amen."*

~~~ Children's Books by Connie Wohlford~~~

Joy Comes to Bethlehem **His Name is Jesus** **He Is The ONE**

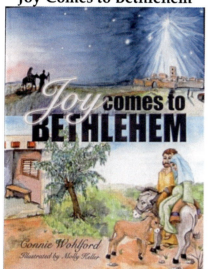
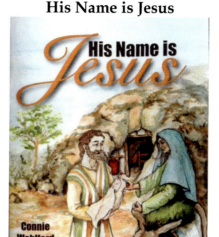
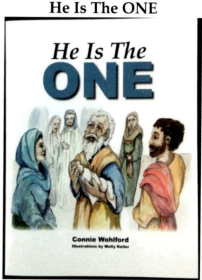

This is a trilogy about infant Jesus, with parallel donkey stories.
Get the set or enjoy each one as a stand-alone book.
Also available- Joy Comes to Bethlehem: A Christmas Play

You're a What?! **Make it a Happy Day**

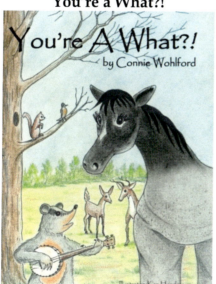

These are stories about that unique rhinokaroarus, Gerald,
and his sidekick, Banjo, the badger.

**To purchase books or for additional information, contact Connie:
author@conniewohlford.com**

Some of these titles are only available through Connie.

Made in the USA
Columbia, SC
25 March 2020